YOUR KNOWLEDGE HAS VALUE

Saima Abedi

Motivating ESL Learners to Refine Writing Skills

GRIN Verlag

Bibliografische Information der Deutschen Nationalbibliothek:

Die Deutsche Bibliothek verzeichnet diese Publikation in der Deutschen National-
bibliografie; detaillierte bibliografische Daten sind im Internet über http://dnb.d-
nb.de/ abrufbar.

Imprint:

Copyright © 2013 GRIN Verlag GmbH
Druck und Bindung: Books on Demand GmbH, Norderstedt Germany
ISBN: 978-3-656-35724-7

This book at GRIN:

http://www.grin.com/en/e-book/208234/motivating-esl-learners-to-refine-writing-
skills

GRIN - Your knowledge has value

Der GRIN Verlag publiziert seit 1998 wissenschaftliche Arbeiten von Studenten, Hochschullehrern und anderen Akademikern als eBook und gedrucktes Buch. Die Verlagswebsite www.grin.com ist die ideale Plattform zur Veröffentlichung von Hausarbeiten, Abschlussarbeiten, wissenschaftlichen Aufsätzen, Dissertationen und Fachbüchern.

Visit us on the internet:

http://www.grin.com/

http://www.facebook.com/grincom

http://www.twitter.com/grin_com

Motivating ESL Learners to Refine Writing Skills

By

Saima Abedi

ESL Teacher for GCE O' Levels

Karachi, Pakistan

ABSTRACT

Motivation is the basic factor for ESL students to excel in the writing class; therefore the role of the teachers is pivotal in writing process. Teachers have to work a lot to raise the level of motivation of the class and sustain it throughout the lesson, as motivated learners work with more interest and intensity. This initiative of teachers and learners can lead to enhancement of writing skills.

INTRODUCTION

Motivation is an essential element of successful language acquisition and is a dynamic process subject to continuous flux (Do¨rnyei, 2001). The word motivation is derived from the word 'motive' which means needs, desires, wants or drives within the individuals. It is the process of stimulating people to actions to accomplish the goals. According to Pintrich & Schunk, (1996) and Williams (1997), motivation, based on the Latin verb for "move," is the force that makes one do something. It is a process that involves goals, physical or mental activity, and is both instigated and sustained.

This paper aims to emphasize on the perennial impact of motivation on ESL learners in the writing class. Firstly, the paper addresses the basic question, what hinders second language learner in writing process and then proposes the strategies that will facilitate the teachers to foster writing motivation in ESL students and refine their written expression.

The suggested approaches will facilitate the teachers to transform the attitude of the unwilling writers to a great extent and remove writer's block. Furthermore, the incorporation of writing prompts, use of music and variety in teaching methodologies will also be discussed. The paper then proceeds to highlight the necessity of modelling, safe writing practice and writing for real purpose to enhance students' writing motivation. Mentors can apply some of the suggested strategies, adapting them in accordance to their own class climate, motivating their students up to optimal level.

RESEARCH

A survey was conducted in which thirty mixed ability learners of various educational institutes, aged 12 to 16 filled a questionnaire (Appendix 1) that was related to writing composition. The responses highlighted ESLs' unwillingness towards writing task and results' analyses revealed that the students are not fully satisfied with their performance as 67% students find writing a pain staking and laborious process.

Almost 57% writers plans a composition before writing yet 50% encounter difficulty in accumulation of ideas and beginning a composition it is also an intricate task for them to find appropriate words to express their thoughts, consequently their composition lacks relevance to the topic and could not stimulate & sustain reader's interest all the time.

1

It was noticed that 77% of these writers prefer to work independently and have no or very less exposure to variety of interaction types (whole class, group work, pair work). 60% of pupils seem to be confident about variation of sentence structure and development of proper links among paragraphs and sentences to maintain a flow (73%). In addition, their work of (57%) displays accuracy of spellings and punctuations; they meet the given word limit (53%) too and conclude the composition aptly (57%). Nonetheless, they are required to emphasis on tenses consistency (50%), usage of speech of figures (33%) to develop vivid imagery and development of reading habit (30%) to get through the barriers in writing.

The students showed their concern about writing classes and suggest that introduction of some activities in composition writing can make the task easier and interesting for them.

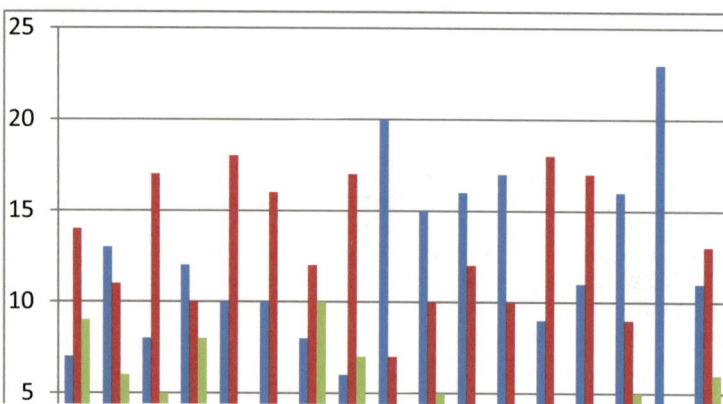

Fig.1 Analysis of Data attained through Questionnaire

DISCUSSION

With great concern it is observed that when teachers initiate a writing task, ESLs show reluctance to write and consider it an ordeal. Here the question arises that why the learners are unmotivated to write and could not show any improvement in their writing skills.

The first reason for being unmotivated is lack of planning. As soon as the teacher announces the topic, students tend to start writing the composition. Planning is the primary stage to gather and organise ideas; however, most of the students skip this step to save time.

Secondly, learners' experience writer's block in the beginning or middle of a composition. Consequently ESLs deviate from the topic and even conclude their compositions abruptly. This often happens because of lack of reading and writing practice which limits students' vocabulary and results in scarcity of appropriate words to express their thoughts freely. Somehow ESLs try to meet the prescribed word count, nonetheless their write ups fail to evoke and maintain readers' interest.

Above all, the monotonous methods to teach writing and working in isolation ebb away learners' interest to such an extent that writing task becomes a reprimand for them. There is a dire need of change of strategies and collaboration for providing a safe and conducive environment to these writers.

2

SUGGESTIONS

Motivation is the indispensable for ESL students especially in the writing classes. Therefore the role of the teachers is pivotal in the writing process. Teachers have to do a lot to raise the level of motivation of the class and sustain it throughout the lesson, as motivated learners work with more interest and intensity.

a) Use of Prompts

The prompts help the learners to improve writing skills to a great level. They have the power to enrich writers' knowledge, boost creativity and enhance critical thinking skills by providing ESL a building block. These starters serve as the foundation of the writing task on which lay the images collected by the writers. The creative juices of the ESL which get dry time to time often need a sprinkle of prompts that can be a puppet, picture, phrase, dialogue, introduction etc. Such support makes the learners comfortable and gives them a direction to let their creative juices flow.

Emphasising on significance of writing prompts, Larry and Katie (2012) state, "Teachers can assess student learning by having students write to a prompt. These prompts can take many forms, such as a question to answer, a statement with which to agree or disagree, a picture to describe, or a response to a text or video clip."

Furthermore, many of the writers acquire their own style in the process of expressing their beliefs, feelings, dreams, hopes and fears, which come to the surface through the use of prompts.
Teacher can easily encourage their students to think and write as there is no right or wrong answer for such prompts. However, if the teacher intends to inculcate something new or unusual then brain storming session is highly recommended. Similarly, the students can also use prompts on their own, to break writer's block which is an obstacle for most of the writers.

It is to be noticed that use of prompts best works when they are selected carefully. The instructors should supply prompts to the learners which are open ended, attractive, age appropriate, culturally accepted and above all related to writer's life.

b) Background Music (BGM)

Background music can be defined as the music played as an inconspicuous addition to any task to build up an atmosphere. In a mundane classroom atmosphere, accompaniment of BMG changes class room climate, making it conducive to learning. It is an easy way to captivate learners' attention and sustain their interest throughout the lesson. Moreover, it enhances creative skills and strengthens imaginative power.

Research has proved the positive effects of BMG on the mood and well being of students, especially soothing music. It has been noticed that relaxing quiet background music can improve behaviour and on-task performance (e.g. Jackson and Owens, 1999; Hallam and Price, 1998) and calming background music has been shown to have a direct impact on biological indicators of stress (e.g. Flaten et al. 2006).

Chris Brewer (1995) in 'Music and Learning' reinforces this idea, "Music stabilizes mental, physical and emotional rhythms to attain a state of deep concentration and focus in which large amounts of content information can be processed and learned."

BMG can be readily incorporated in the lesson by either using it while the students write, to increase their concentration or as an indicator to mark the beginning or ending of any class activity. Nonetheless Griffin, M. Points out that here the most important factor is the choice of music, as "certain components have more effect on our mood and physiology than others. In particular, tonality, tempo, pitch and texture all play an important role in affecting our mood. For example music of a major tonality is recognised to be happier and more positive than minor music." Thus the teacher should be careful in selection of the music. It is better to involve students in this selection process and give preference to their choice.

c) Real Purpose for Writing

According to Kelly (2006), "When students understand the real-world purposes for writing (instead of simply writing to meet the next school requirement) they begin to internalize the relevance of writing, and more important, they develop an understanding that writing is an important skill to carry into adulthood. When the students begin to understand this relevance, their writing improves."

Real purpose and real audience do matter in motivation of writers. The main reason for the lack of students' interest in writing task is assigning a topic or supplying a prompt which has no connection with the real lives of the learners. Consequently, the task becomes boring and the learners give up quickly.

On the other hand, if students are asked to describe any of their belonging without which they will be gloomy, or email to friend informing how they spent their weekend, compose a letter to editor telling about the miseries of students' lives, or debate about the necessity of mobile phones in school, write directions of their house; certainly, none of the learner will be stuck at any point. Brimming with ideas, they will write enthusiastically, without teachers' assistance.

To sum up, writing with an aim and objective facilitates the writers to use prior knowledge, understand or analyse the present situation and express ideas effectively. Moreover, learners will have sufficient vocabulary to express their thoughts freely as they would be well acquainted with the theme and scenario.

d) Modelling

In teaching, model is defined as a thing used as an example to follow. Eggen and Kauchak's Educational Psychology (2001) defines modelling as "changes in people that result from observing the actions of others."

Heather (2008) in his article explains that modelling is an instructional strategy in which the teacher demonstrates a new concept or approach to learning and students learn by observing. According to Albert (1986), the originator of social learning theory and the theory of self-efficacy, "Modelling is an effective instructional strategy in that it allows students to observe the teacher's thought processes. Using this type of instruction, teachers engage students in imitation of particular behaviours that encourage learning."

Use of model compositions and the act of modelling both are of utmost importance in ESL classroom. Supply of sample essays or letters provides students some useful reading material for scaffolding as they start focusing on the given theme. Simultaneously, learners are exposed to appropriate structures along with the opportunity to consolidate theme based vocabulary. This step is vital to inspire and influence writers especially those students who require continual guidance of teacher in order to write coherently.

Similarly, whenever teachers assign a task to students they should also perform that task to make the students' understand what and how to do. In such a way, the learners will observe the teachers' manners and gradually attain a control over their own behaviour.

e) Safe Journaling

A journal is a blank notebook that is used to pour down thoughts and feelings. Journaling is a technique that is adopted by many writers as a personal and safe way to hone writing skills. Teachers can recommend the learners to maintain a daily or free writing journal and set 15 or 20 minutes to write in it every day or jot down ideas that flash in their mind anytime.

Safe Journaling offers multitude of benefits related to physical and mental wellbeing of the person. It can remove writers' blocks and allow their thoughts to flow freely. Moreover, it curtails down stress, clarifies thoughts and feelings. It also helps in generating, expanding and preserving ideas by enhancing creative and observational skills. Furthermore, it also provides the opportunity to analyze mistakes and track progress.

Spack and Sadow (1983) argued that ungraded, uncorrected journals can provide a non threatening way for learners to express themselves in written English. Winner (1992) studied how journals can help to change negative attitudes among English as a Second Langusage (ESL) teacher in training towards teaching writing.

Keeping in mind the countless benefits of safe journaling, teachers can allocate some time daily or weekly for free writing in the class. Students should be guided to write anything that comes to their mind, forgetting about errors of spelling, punctuation, sentence structure or coherence of ideas.

f) Collaboration

Collaboration, which means working together like a team to achieve a goal, has been a source of motivation especially in writing class. As writing process becomes a shared goal and objective; therefore students in collaboration, accept challenges, increasing their creativity and productivity. They work in a form of a group that is usually comprised of four to six members. The students share their knowledge, undergo discussions, negotiations and finally reach consensus. In the writing classes, where collaborative or co-operative teaching is practised, the role of teacher changes from instructor to facilitator or organiser, giving rise to a student centred class.

The benefits of collaborative learning optimises when mixed ability groups are formed by the teacher. In such a way, the strong members of the group share their strengthens and enhance leadership qualities, where as the weaker members are also accountable for their work individually, so they develop their weaker skills by seeking guidance from the peers, in a safe environment.

Emphasising on the significance of collaboration in writing class, Gocsik, K. (2004) states, "Students must overcome isolation in order to learn to write. Collaborative learning exercises—such as peer review workshops, collaborative research assignments, group presentations, collaborative papers, discussion groups, and so on—are important components of our writing classrooms because they encourage active learning, giving students the opportunity to become more deeply engaged with their writing, and with one another."

However, according to Spring, M. (1997), "Writing is a complex, open-ended task, there are many ways of stating meaning. With multiple authors, this adds to the complexity. The acts of collaboration and writing as they relate to collaborative authoring include: establishing an agenda or goal of the collaboration effort, identifying writing tasks and dividing those tasks among group members, tracking individual idea generation, defining rules for document management, identifying roles for group members, communicating ideas, and managing conflict. Collaborative authoring, therefore, requires effective communication between members of the writing group."

Therefore in his article 'Collaborative Writing', Spring identified seven organizational patterns for collaborative authoring which were based on the results of the study conducted by Ede and Lunsford. These patterns are:

1. the team plans and outlines the task, then each writer prepares his/her part and the group compiles the individual parts, and revises the whole document as needed;
2. the team plans and outlines the writing task, then one member prepares a draft, the team edits and revises the draft;
3. one member of the team plans and writes a draft, the group revises the draft;
4. one person plans and writes the draft, then one or more members revises the draft without consulting the original authors;
5. the group plans and writes the draft, one or more members revise the draft without consulting the original authors;
6. one person assigns the tasks, each member completes the individual task, one person compiles and revises the document;
7. one dictates, another transcribes and edits.

Sometimes collaborative learning also gives rise to disciplinary issues in classroom. For such activities, the managerial role of teachers should be stronger than usual. Firstly, the groups should be even, in accordance to the number of members and their abilities. Secondly, every group member should assume the given responsibility religiously; for that, badges should be provided to the students to remind them the part they have to play in the group, for instance: Writer/ Editor/ Speaker or Narrator/ Presenter Etc. Such clarifications at the earliest prevent many conflicts that could mar the efficacy of collaborative learning. Thirdly, the teachers need to be observant and monitor student's individual performance meticulously plus provide assistance if required.

Team self assessment, peer rating and random presenter selection can further enhance students' individual accountability and ensure active learning, in addition to accomplishment of goal.

g) Variety of Teaching Strategies

Teaching writing to ESL is challenging and time consuming. However, ESL instructors can enliven writing classes by diversifying teaching strategies. This will not only make writing task easy and exciting yet assist students to refine their writing skills. For instance, teaching writing to learners with a limited vocabulary can be a daunting task; thus providing a word bank, taking a quiz, supply of sample essay can enrich vocabulary and facilitates writing task.

Henard. and Leprince in "The Path to Quality Teaching in Higher Education" quoted Meyers and Jones (1993) who define active learning as learning environments that allow "students to talk and listen, read, write, and reflect as they approach course content through problem-solving exercises, informal small groups, simulations, case studies, role playing, and other activities - all of which require students to apply what they are learning". Here the use of role-plays can add variety to ESL writing lesson and turn students into active learners.

Highlighting the significance of role play, Tompkins (1998) states, "It encourages thinking and creativity, lets students develop and practice language and behavioural skills in a relatively nonthreatening setting, and can create the motivation and involvement necessary for learning to occur." As role play provides the student a general situation with suggested ideas therefore students get the opportunity to practice dialogue writing in a safe environment.

To generate multitude of ideas and stimulate thinking, teachers can conduct brainstorming before writing session. However, use of graphic organizers to order ideas can aid learners in proper paragraphing and maintenance of relevance. Venn diagram, Five W's Chart, Time line and Story Map are few of such examples.

Furthermore, as writing with an aim is the best motivator hence some interactive games should be incorporated in the lesson plan to trigger students' observational and thinking skills. Manish & Yogesh (2009), reinforce this idea and state, "Teachers can provide students with a wonderful learning experience by integrating games into their lessons."

The content based games captivate students' attention right from the beginning of the lesson; cultivate a learning atmosphere and motivate the writers towards writing task. In this regard, Mystery Objects, Guessing and Code Breaking games provide equal chance for writing and fun; as a result teachers easily achieve the learning objectives.

Conclusion

ESL instructors are quite enthusiastic and motivated to develop writing skills and improve their students' performance. However, it is time to enthuse this willingness among students to polish their writing skills. Learners too need to understand the power of writing as it controls their lives and influences their future.

References

Bandura, A. (1986) Social Foundations of Thought and Action: A Social Cognitive. Prentice-Hall Inc: New Jersey.

Brewer, Chris. (1995) Music and Learning: Seven Ways to Use Music in the Classroom. Tequesta, Florida: LifeSounds

Eggen, Pand Don K. (2001) Educational Psychology: Classroom Connections. 5th ed Macmillan: New York.

Flaten, M.A., Asli, O. and Simonsen, T. (2006) The Effect of Stress on Absorption of Acetaminophen. *Psychopharmocology*, 185(4), 471-8.

Ferlazzo, L & Sypnieski, K. H. (2012) The ESL / ELL Teacher's Survival Guide. John Wiley & Sons, Inc. USA.

Gallagher, K. (2006) Teaching Adolescent Writing. Stenhouse Publishers: USA.

Hallam, S. and Price, J. (1998) Can the Use of Background Music Improve the Behaviour and Academic Performance of Children with Emotional and Behavioural Difficulties? *British Journal of Special Education*, 25(2), 88-91.

Jackson, J.T. and Owens, J.L. (1999) A Stress Management Classroom Tool for Teachers Of Children with BD. *Intervention in School and Clinic,* 35(2), 74-78.

Pintrich, P. R., & Schunk, D. H. (1996) Motivation in Education: Theory, Research and Applications. Prentice-Hall Inc: New Jersey.

Spack, R. & Sadow, C. (1983) Learner-teacher working journals in ESL freshman composition. TESOL Quarterly, 17 (4), 575-593.

Tompkins, P. (1998) Role Playing and Simulation. The Internet TESL Journal, 4(8).

Vyas M. A. & Patel, Y. L., ed., (2009) Teaching English as a Second Language. PHI Learning Private Limited: New Delhi.

Williams, M. B., Robert. (1997) Psychology for Language Teachers: A Social Constructivist View. Cambridge: New York.

Winer, L. (1992) "Spinach to Chocolate": Changing Awareness and Attitudes in ESL Writing Teachers. TESOL Quarterly, 26(1), 57-80.

Internet:

Aberra, N. The Benefits of Writing Prompts. Retrieved 9th Oct 2012 from http://youngandwriterly.wordpress.com/2010/09/14/the-benefits-of-writing-prompts/

Coffey, H. Modeling. Retrieved 4th Nov 2012 from http://www.learnnc.org/lp/pages/4697

Hallam, S. The Effects of Background Music on Health and Well-Being. Retrieved 7th Oct'12 from www.icanteach.co.uk/open-resource/resource-id=214

Griffin, M. Background music in the classroom. Retrieved 24th Nov 2012 from http://www.musiceducationworld.com/files/Background%20music%20in%20classrooms.pdf

Gocsik, K. Collaborative Learning/Learning with Peers. Retrieved 24th Nov 2012 from http://www.dartmouth.edu/~writing/materials/faculty/methods/collaborative.shtml

Hand, L. Role Plays in the ESL Classroom. Retrieved 3rd Oct 2012 from http://www.learnenglish.de/Teachers/roleplays.htm

Henard, F. and Leprince, S. The Path to Quality Teaching in Higher Education. Retrieved 24th Nov 2012 from http://essaybank.degree-essays.com/anthropology/importance-of-effective-teaching-methodologies.php#ixzz2DAFmuqWu

Kelly, C. A Review of Traditional and Current Theories of Motivation in ESL. Retrieved 24th July 2012from http://www.osaka-gu.ac.jp/php/kelly/papers/motivation.html

Landsberger, J. (n.d.). Citing Websites. In Study Guides and Strategies. Retrieved May 13, 2005, from http://www.studygs.net/citation.htm.

Latumahina, D. The Benefits of Keeping a Journal. Retrieved 9th Oct' 12from http://www.lifeoptimizer.org/2009/08/04/keeping-a-journal/

Marten, M. Five Reasons to Use Writing Prompts. Retrieved 3rd Oct 2012 from http://voices.yahoo.com/five-reasons-writing-prompts-141711.html

Mascle, D. Ten Reasons Why You Should Use Writing Prompts. Retrieved 9th Oct 2012 from http://www.archetypewriting.com/articles/writing/usePrompts.htm

Norton, B. Using Journals in Second Language Research and Teaching. Retrieved 4th Nov 2012 from http://educ.ubc.ca/faculty/norton/Smoke%20(1998)%20-%20Using%20journals%20in%20second%20language%20research%20and%20teaching.pdf

Purcell, M. The Health Benefits Of Journaling. Retrieved 9th Oct' 12 from http://psychcentral.com/lib/2006/the-health-benefits-of-journaling/

Smith, E. The Effect of a Writing Journal on Writing Skills. Retrieved 9th Oct' 12from http://www.ehow.com/facts_5767378_effect-writing-journal-writing-skills.html#ixzz28mXkRAnH

Spring, M. Collaborative Writing. Retrieved 24th Nov 2012 from http://www.sis.pitt.edu/~spring/cas/node31.html

Appendix 1

Name: _____   Class: _____   Date: _____

Questionnaire on Writing Practice

Tick off the grids keeping your present situation in mind:

S. No.	Question	Often	Sometimes	Never
1	Are you satisfied with your performance in composition paper?			
2	Do you think writing composition is a laborious process?			
3	Do you plan your composition before writing?			
4	Do you find it hard to gather ideas?			
5	Do you address the topic with consistent relevance?			
6	Do your compositions stimulate and sustain the interest of the readers?			
7	Is writing introduction of a composition, the most difficult task for you?			
8	Do you face trouble in finding appropriate words to express your thoughts?			
9	Are your sentences and paragraphs properly linked with one another?			
10	Do your compositions display variety of sentence structure?			
11	Do you retain appropriate tenses consistency in your writing task?			
12	Are your spellings and punctuation accurate?			
13	Do you use figures of speech to make your compositions interesting?			
14	Do you conclude your compositions aptly?			
15	Do you usually meet the prescribed word limit for continuous writing?			
16	Do you complete your writing assignments independently?			
17	Have you ever tried to enhance your writing skills yourself?			
18	Have you ever read your friends' compositions?			
19	Do you read books and newspapers?			
20	Should writing composition be activity-based?			